FAMILY
DAY CARE
ACTIVITIES

FROM A TO Z

**Developmentally
Appropriate Activities for Preschool–age
Children**

by Joan Prestine

Fearon Teacher Aids
Carthage, Illinois

Illustrated by Elaine Kallas

ISBN 0-8224-3073-8

Printed in the United States of America
1. 9 8 7 6 5 4

Contents

Introduction

So you're a family day care provider now. For most of the day, you're responsible for other people's children. Keep in mind that family day care is regulated by law and that licensing and registration requirements must be fulfilled. However, once you have established your home as a licensed day care, you will be called on to make decisions that the parents would usually make. Those decisions will include planning meals, discipline, and even the activities that fill the children's day. It's a lot of hours and a long, long day for you and the children. How can you make those hours special? How can you make the day enjoyable for the children without making your day stressful and harried? This book contains a wealth of simple, easy-to-use activities from A to Z, which will help you make those hours fun, enjoyable, and educational. The topical index in the back of the book will help you quickly find a specific type of activity, whether it be painting, woodworking, or kitchen fun.

The following is a brief summary of the kinds of activities presented and some tips for making the activities a successful experience for you and the children.

Arts and Crafts

A successful craft is one a child can complete without frustration. I have found several simple crafts that children have the dexterity to create and can enjoy the end result pridefully. Remember, preschool children are just developing fine motor coordination. The success of a project will depend on its simplicity. And this simplicity makes preparation and cleanup easier for you. Children are just now experiencing the basics of coloring, painting, and gluing. They are enthralled with these activities and want to try them over and over again to perfect their skills. Before beginning a project, gather your supplies together. Decide where the craft will be assembled. Cut a piece of vinyl large enough to cover your table or work area. Demonstrate how to make the project for the children. Then respect their efforts and help only when needed. Children make their major move toward independence between ages one and three. Exploration expands their independence and children learn through their curiosity.

Cooking

Carefully chosen kitchen activities can be fun for preschoolers. Make it clear to the children that they will all help with everything— including cleanup. Kitchen cleanup for children is different than for adults. They love to play in water and wash and wash and wash that plate. So, let them. Not only is it fun, but children feel important when they do adult work. The children feel a sense of responsibility if they carry over their own dishes, rinse them, and put them into the dishwasher or on the counter. There are certain safety rules that adults and children should be aware of. An adult should always stay in the kitchen with the children while they are cooking. When the children want to see what is happening on the counter, have them stand on kitchen chairs. Place the back of a chair to the counter so that a child will be able to hold on. Only the adult turns the stove on or off. If you are cooking on top of the stove, make sure all pot handles are turned to the back of the stove. This prevents children from knocking the pan off the stove and getting burned. Don't use recipes that call for boiling syrup or hot oil.

Drama

The child with an active imagination has a hundred friends and a thousand games. When children are left alone, they often dive into the world of fantasy. Children love to be someone else. They act out what happens in their own homes and what happens in the outside world. They move into the role of Mommy, Daddy, or other people who are important to them. Imagination allows them to become teachers, astronauts, race car drivers, or garbage collectors. Or, children revert back to babyhood in order to handle fears about visiting the dentist, a move, divorce, or other situations they find difficult to handle.

Exercise

Some of the activities listed in this book are simple exercises that will allow the children to use their muscles. Exercise is important for the success of your day care. With exercise, children will sleep better and cry less. I joined in and did the exercises with the children. Not only did I set the example, I also got my exercise for the day!

Music and Songs

Music definitely has a place in your day care. You may feel inadequate because you don't play an instrument or sing well. Don't worry. You can put on a record, play a tape, or clap your hands. And children simply don't notice if you sing off-key. Smile and sing with confidence. They'll think you're as good as the people on TV! Music can satisfy many moods. If the children are overexcited, have them lie on the floor and quietly listen to soft music. If they seem a little down or draggy, play upbeat music to give them a lift in spirit. Music can also be used as a physical release. Encourage children to move and dance in rhythm to the music. And children enjoy acting out songs. This can be done with hand signs or complete body motion.

Reading

Reading quality books to children can greatly enhance their day with you. Use books to quiet children down after a busy, exciting activity. Gather them all together on the floor or on a cozy couch, and read a story aloud with expression and enthusiasm. Choose books that will delight the children, expose them to a new concept, or help meet an emotional need. A list of suggested books for preschool-age children appears at the end of this book and can serve as a guide in helping you choose appropriate reading material.

Toys

Toys are always enjoyed by preschoolers. However, it's a good idea to put away all toys and games that have small pieces. Through trial and error, I found that a group of children doesn't have the attention span to concentrate on anything intricate. If children are given a compli-cated toy or puzzle, interest usually wanes and they don't want to pick it up. Therefore, the

10

pieces get broken, lost, or put in the wrong place. This aggravates the child who owns the toy, or the provider who has to sort through the mess. A toy that involves the child is more valuable than a toy a child looks at. For example, a rag doll isn't as pretty as a storybook doll, but the participation level is much higher. I discovered that as a child becomes bored or frustrated with a toy, it is time to put it away and direct him or her to another activity before the temper begins to fly. Look for sturdy, nontoxic, nonflammable toys. They should have smooth edges with no pins, buttons, springs, or screws that a child could pull loose. Choose a toy made of wood or strong plastic. Avoid toys made with glass or other potentially harmful materials.

Woodworking

I discovered there were few things that generated as much excitement among the children as wood scraps, a hammer, and nails. Not a master carpenter, I could still give three-year-olds a few hints on how to wield a hammer and some lessons on basic woodworking skills. If you don't have wood scraps at home, visit your local lumberyard. They are only too happy to let children, and even adults, clean out scrap barrels free of charge. If you are also going to buy tools, avoid toy tool sets for children. Most of these are flimsily made and lead to frustration. Since children handle big objects more easily than little ones, they'll have greater success developing a few basic skills with real tools. While the children work, stay close. Be firm with the children about proper use of the tools. If there is deliberate misuse, remove the tools.

Hints
for a Successful Day

Structure

When the children arrive in your home, it may take them a while to unwind. If they are overexuberant, read a book or turn on the television to a children's program for about half an hour. The children may feel a bit apprehensive about being separated from their parents. Half an hour or so after arriving, they usually wander to an activity area to play with toys.

Between playtimes, provide children with a midmorning snack, a lunch, and a nap time if necessary. For each three-hour period, except during lunch and nap time, you will probably want to tentatively plan two or three activities. But if the children are happy to continue an activity that you felt would only last fifteen minutes, leave them alone. Remember, your main goal is to have the children play well together in relative peace and quiet.

Through much experimentation I learned to combine quiet activities with active ones. With only quiet activities, the energy levels of the children climb and they become rowdy. On the other hand, if you plan three hours of active play, the children will become keyed up and will not calm down. Alternate quiet activities with active ones so that the children have a chance to use up their energy and then calm down. It is also better to stop an activity while children are still enjoying it, not after interest has waned. If you wait until interest has subsided, the mood of the children is generally more negative than positive. Then you will have to deal with their temperaments along with organizing a new activity.

Weather permitting, it's to everyone's advantage to do as many of the suggested activities outside as possible. Try to have at least one activity outside each day. The advantages of outdoor play are obvious: cleanup is much easier, you don't have to worry about breakage, and the children enjoy the freedom of being outside.

The family day care home does not need to be run like a school. Although it is a good plan to have a potential agenda for each day, flexibility is also important so that the children's needs and interests can be met.

Supervision

The key to success is to remain within earshot but to avoid constant interaction. If I sat in a chair and watched the chidren play, I was inviting them to interact with me. When I was quietly doing nothing, the children thought they had my undivided attention and wanted me to play with them. I began to do other projects around the house such as folding laundry, making beds, or sewing. I was within their sight and close enough, so that I could hear all that was going on in case I was needed. The children played more freely with each other and with the toys available to them than when I supervised too closely.

Therefore, let children do as much for

themselves as possible: put their own coats on, go to the bathroom, wash their hands, get drinks, pick up toys, and clean up spills.

Separation

Many times children will be apprehensive about being left without their parents. Talk with distressed children and reassure them that parents will be back at the determined time. A phone call to a child from the parent during the day can help ease anxious feelings. Encourage the parent to call and say everything is OK.

If time allows the parent to stay for a while on the first few days, the following suggestion might be helpful. When the child is comfortable, the parent should go to another part of the house where he or she is out of sight but within earshot. As soon as the child is involved, the parent can come in and tell the child that he or she is going for a ten-minute walk outside. The parent should return in ten minutes, not thirty. As the child becomes more confident that the parent is really coming back, the length of time absent can be extended. The parent should always tell the child goodbye and how long he or she will be gone and never sneak out when the child is busy. The parent should strive to maintain a trust. If the parent sneaks out, the child will feel anxious and betrayed. It may take a while, but the child will let go.

Sharing

Sharing toys and possessions can be a difficult problem for children. It was also tough on me when I had to referee these disputes.

If you as the provider have a child who will be participating in the activities, you need to make that child aware that other children are coming to play not only with him or her but also with his or her toys. And please, put your child's favorite toy away before everyone arrives. This will save a lot of hurt feelings if the child chooses not to share it. The visiting children should be told that the toys belong to the host and that they should help put everything back before going home.

Remind children that sharing can be difficult, but everyone can work together teaching each other how to share better. The kitchen timer can solve many a dispute. It's an effective means of giving everyone unbiased, equal time with a favorite toy. If several children want to play with the same toy, set the timer for three minutes, or whatever is appropriate, and tell each child he or she will have an equal turn.

Distraction by giving each child a different toy also helps. Another method you might try is to sit down on the floor, so that everyone is of equal height, and explain how friends share toys.

Discipline

When it is time to interact to solve a crisis, do not stand with your hand on your hip, pointing a finger and wagging your tongue. I sat on the floor and talked to the children. I got their undivided attention if I sat or lay on the floor so that we were all on the same level, and the children loved it. Children will get the feeling you are talking with them rather than at them. No one likes to be talked down to. Children may tune you out. Try to remember, in order to get their attention, talk *with* the children, not *at* them.

If the children are too young to reason with, sing a song or read a book to distract them. You will generally find things beginning to flow more smoothly if you remove the children from the sour situation. There is nothing like the distraction of a new activity to help small children over the bumps they are bound to have.

A child may become aggressive. In this case it may be necessary for you to take stronger action and have the child sit in a chair until calm. In a firm, positive statement, tell the child he or she may get down when able to play properly with the other children.

Hitting among the children should not be allowed. Children should be encouraged to learn verbal skills in order to handle conflict.

Snacks and Lunchtime

This can be a prime time to talk about nutrition. According to nutritional studies, a balanced diet can raise an IQ twenty points, while an improper, unbalanced diet can cause retardation. Offer children drinks and foods that are nutritious, and explain why it's better to eat a balanced diet. Milk, juice, and water are appropriate drinks. Children enjoy small snacks such as raisins, nuts, crackers, or little chunks of cheese. Fruit, carrots, or other crunchy vegetables are also good to nibble on.

If the weather permits, serve food outside. All messes and spills stay outside, plus the children enjoy being outdoors.

A tea party is always a favorite of children. All children enjoy miniature dish sets, so even the boys love a tea party. Let the children get the dishes out and set the table. Remember the napkins, since each child should be responsible for his or her own spills. Fill the pitcher or teapot partially full with milk, juice, or water, and let everyone try pouring and passing. If you have a younger group, water is best. When children spill, they can learn to mop up, too. Allow children to pass around the snacks and put a few on their tiny plates. This also provides an excellent opportunity to introduce and practice using good manners. Children can learn to pass to the next person, instead of reaching or passing across the table. Encourage children to say "please," "thank you," and "no, thank you."

Lunchtime routines can vary from a family-style meal served at a table to a picnic on the grass. Children can help with the table setting, food preparation, and cleanup.

Cleanup

Everyone should help in the cleanup process. It's a habit that needs to be formed even in young children. They like to do "grown-up" jobs, so allow the children to help wash dishes, sweep, and vacuum while under your supervision. Make a game out of cleanup time. Set the timer and see if everyone can help pick up all the toys before the timer rings. Label shelves and boxes where toys belong, and cleanup can be turned into a matching game. Everything has a special place. Try singing favorite songs while you and the children are cleaning up. It passes the time more quickly and can be a happy way to end the day.

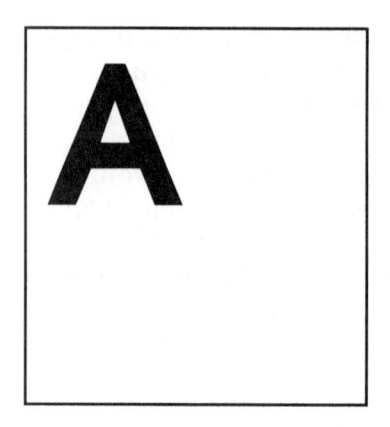

Air Balls

The pride the children will feel upon completion of this project is worth every bit of the work. Blow up a balloon for each child. Attach a 6" string to each balloon. Cut six 12" lengths of yarn for each balloon. Dip the yarn into a bowl of watered down white glue. Wrap the yarn lengthwise around the balloons. The pieces must cross at the top and bottom of the balloons. Hang the balloons to dry for about 45 minutes. While the wet yarn is drying on the balloons, have the children help clean up. When the yarn is dry, give the children pins and let them pop the balloons. When the scraps are pulled out of the yarn, the children will have rigid air balls.

Aluminum Foil Dolls

The children can create their own dolls out of aluminum foil. Cut a 10" piece of foil. Roll the foil into a cylinder. Pinch it in the center for a waist and then a little higher for a neck. Press the foil above the neck into a ball for a head. Wrap a pipe cleaner around the neck with the ends extending out to form the arms. Children can dress their dolls by cutting additional lengths of aluminum foil and designing dresses, pants, or shirts.

Angels

While lying on the floor, children stretch their arms straight above their heads. Their legs are straight out and close together. Have children open and close their arms and then open and close their legs. Have them try doing both at once!

Ants on a Log

Separate, wash, and cut celery stalks into 4" pieces. Have children use blunt knives and spread peanut butter inside the celery stalks. Have them place raisins in a row on top of the peanut butter and then enjoy eating their masterpieces.

Avocado Tree

Clean an avocado seed. Place four toothpicks in a circle around the avocado seed about halfway down. Place the rounded end of the seed in a glass of water. Rest the toothpicks on the rim of the glass. Place the container in a cool, dark area such as a closet until you see some growth, which is usually in two to four weeks. Then place the seed in a sunny area and add water when necessary. It is intriguing to watch the bottom of the seed sprout roots and the top grow into a tree.

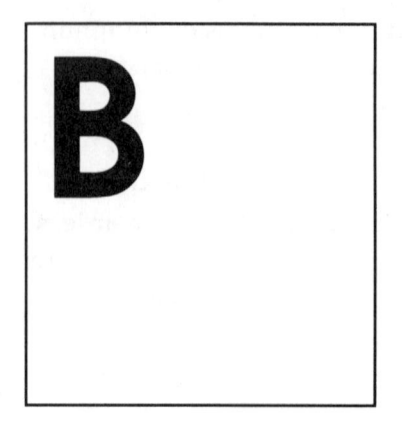

Bag People

Children always like puppets. They are fun to make and lend themselves to a great game of pretend. Leave paper bags folded and have the children slip their hands into the bags with their fingers over the inside folds. The flat bottom of each bag becomes the head. The head moves as the child's fingers wiggle back and forth. The moving fold resembles the mouth. Cut eyes, nose, and a mouth out of construction paper and glue them onto the bag, or draw a face with crayons. Yarn works well for hair.

Balance Beam

Use any long piece of wood (a two-by-four works especially well). Let children practice walking on the beam. Then suggest pretending they are tightrope walkers. Have the children try walking backward, hopping over the beam, straddling it, or jumping off. Follow the Leader is a fun game to play on the beam. Have one child think of a movement to do when crossing the beam, and have others copy the movement as they go across one at a time.

Band

A homemade band can be more fun than one with authentic instruments. An empty oatmeal carton can be a drum. Hit a spoon on an empty pan, lid, or coffee can to make different sounds. And don't overlook the wonders of pot lids used as crashing cymbals! The children will love the band, and you can wear earmuffs.

Basketball

This is a toddler variation of the real thing. Line boxes in varying distances from a point where the children have been told to stand. Children try throwing a ball into one of the boxes. Depending on how easily the ball goes in, you may want to move the boxes farther away to increase the difficulty.

Batik

Four-year-olds are able to make batiks under your supervision. Have children color designs with crayons on white handkerchiefs or pieces of white sheet. Have them press hard while creating their art. The pressure forces the wax into the fabric. Dampen two paper towels. Lay the fabric between the two wet towels, and iron until the paper is dry and the melted crayon has set.

Beanbag

A beanbag is more fun than a ball because it stops right where it lands. Using chalk, draw targets on the sidewalk, and have children throw beanbags so that they will land inside the target shapes.

Blocks

After carefully constructing architectural achievements, children can watch their master-pieces tumble down during a giant "earthquake" that someone caused by quietly kicking the blocks. That's OK; the children can quickly rebuild, in order to experience another "earthquake."

Blowing Bubbles

This activity should be done outside. Buy small plastic jars of bubble solution, and allow children to blow through the small hoops provided in each jar. Sometimes blowing is hard for small children, and you might suggest that they wave the hoops after dipping them carefully in the solution.

Bowling

I didn't buy a bowling set. I stood the children's blocks up and found a rubber ball. Bowling requires a combination of block building and ball rolling. Most of the children have never bowled, so the fun of this is letting them set up the blocks in many original patterns. Some may line the blocks up, while others may group them or build towers to knock down. Start rolling the ball in a position not too far from the blocks, and as the children get better they can move farther back. It's not necessary to keep score.

Boxes

Boxes are a special treat for young children. Go to your local grocery store, and ask for sturdy brown boxes. Give each child a box. The activities with boxes are endless. Let children paint, color, glue, or do whatever they want with their boxes. Children can climb in them and use them as houses, cars, trains, boats, or beds. Or, they can just tumble around in the boxes. Children spend hours inventing various games with their boxes. They play train, house, Follow the Leader, and Peek-a-Boo. They may choose to play with their boxes as a group or individually. Sometimes a child may need to be alone, and a box can provide a place of solitude. Also, at some point in the day, each child needs a rest. The children don't resist quiet time if they stay in their boxes. They don't equate their boxes to their bedrooms or nap time. The marvel of boxes is that at the end of the day or week, you can send them home with the children, store them in the garage, or put them in the garbage. You can have hours of fun with boxes, limited only by the child's imagination and at no cost to you.

Broken Toy Collage

Keep small broken toys or pieces of toys. The children can glue them on pieces of cardboard to make interesting collages. Have the children color or paint the cardboard before gluing the materials to it. Due to the weight of the toys, you might find it necessary to help the children use a super-strength adhesive glue or epoxy found in your grocery store.

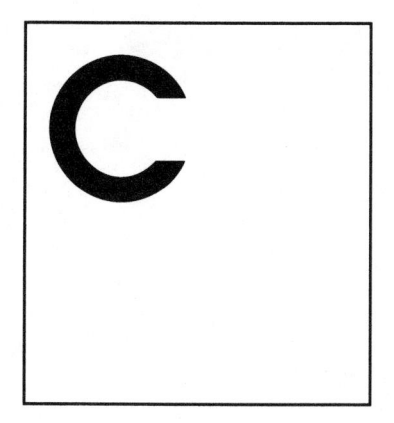

Candles

I found the children were exceedingly proud of their candles. They couldn't quite believe they had made them. Candles are fun because they have a function and last a long time. Remove labels from juice or soup cans. Make sure there are no sharp edges. Tie a string to the middle of a nail for each can. Make sure the strings are longer than the length of the cans. Fasten a paper clip or safety pin to the bottom of each string. This acts as a weight. Then lay the nails across the tops of the cans. In an old pan, melt leftover candles at medium heat until they have completely melted. *You pour the melted wax* into each child's can. Allow the wax to harden. Clip off the nails. The candles may be removed from the cans or left inside. If they are left inside, the children may want to cover the cans with construction paper or fabric. The children can glue lightweight objects onto the cans or color them.

Candy Clay

Here is the recipe for an edible sculpture:

1/3 cup margarine
1/3 cup corn syrup
1/2 tablespoon salt
1 box powdered sugar
food coloring

Mix above ingredients. Create it, mold it, and eat it.

Cardboard Puzzles

Have each child color an original picture on a piece of cardboard. Cut the cardboard into three or four pieces. Have the children sit in a circle and put all their puzzle pieces in the center of the circle. Mix all the pieces together. The children find the pieces to their own puzzles and put them together again.

Cars on Tracks

These cars are fun for boys or girls. All ages enjoy watching the small cars fly up, down, and around the plastic track.

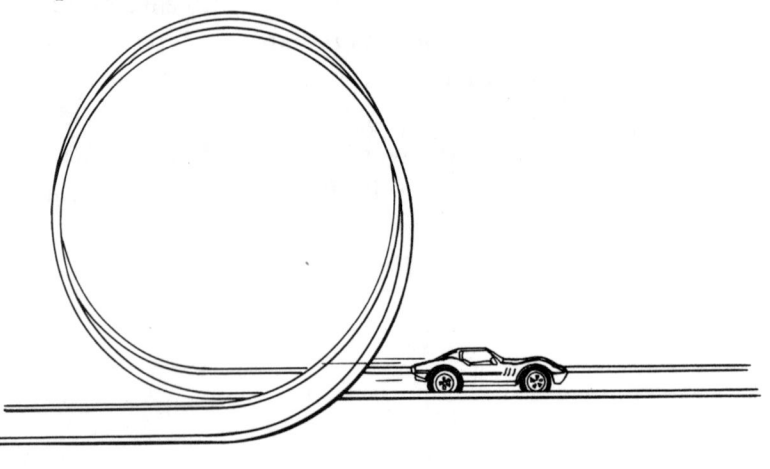

Cat and Mouse

This is a quiet game. One child is chosen to be the cat. Have that child close his or her eyes and sit on a chair fifteen feet in front of the other children. The cat's back is toward the other players. The cat's mouse, which is an eraser or small book, is placed behind the chair. Choose one child to try to sneak up to the cat and touch the "mouse" without the cat hearing. If the cat hears someone coming, he or she turns around and says, "Meow!" Then the player goes back to the group, and another child has a chance to out-smart the cat and touch the "mouse." If success-ful, this child is the next cat.

Cereal Candy

2 1/4 cups semisweet chocolate bits
4 cups cereal

Melt the chocolate in a double boiler or microwave. Add cereal and mix well. Drop by teaspoonfuls onto waxed paper and allow to harden. Or, spread in greased shallow pan to a 1/4" thickness. Cool and cut into squares. Makes about 34 small pieces.

Cereal Collage

The brightly colored breakfast cereals are perfect for a collage, and the children can snack while they work.

Colored Flowers

These novel creations are a breeze to make. Add a few drops of food coloring to a glass of water. Soak flower stems in the colored water, and in a few hours everyone can watch the flowers change colors.

Cookies

Children love nothing more than creating something and then eating the creations. This activity is fun for children three years and older. The following recipe may be used with cookie cutters or as drop cookies.

In a bowl, mix:
3 cups sifted flour
1/2 teaspoon salt
1/2 teaspoon baking powder

In another bowl, cream:
1/2 cup shortening
1/2 cup sugar
2 eggs
1/2 teaspoon vanilla

Mix both bowls of ingredients, and add 3 tablespoons of milk. Press dough into a firm roll. Chill dough in the refrigerator for at least an hour. When the dough is firm, roll it flat on a lightly floured board until it is 1/4" thick.

Cut out cookies with cookie cutters, or let the children drop spoonfuls of dough on a greased cookie sheet. Bake at 375° F for 7–8 minutes. Remember to put children on cleanup detail.

When I planned cookie-making for children, this was the only activity organized for the morning. Right after the children arrived, they mixed the ingredients. I followed this activity with something that burned up excess energy, so when the dough had chilled, they were ready to sit quietly while creating.

After the cookies cooled, I let the children decorate them. Sprinkles and other fun cake-decorating items found at the grocery store allowed for true works of art.

Frosting:
1 cup sifted confectioners' sugar
1/4 teaspoon salt
1/2 teaspoon vanilla
1 1/2 tablespoons cream or water
food coloring

This recipe will frost 3–5 dozen cookies.

Cornmeal

Place cornmeal in a large bowl on a tray. Give the children bowls, spoons, cups, gelatin molds, and other small cooking utensils. Let them mix, fill, and pour. To an adult this sounds simple, almost silly, but children can do it almost endlessly.

Crystal Garden

These gardens go through an intricate change, which fascinates children. Be sure to set them up out of the children's reach because of the harmful chemicals in the containers. In a shallow dish or pie plate, place 3 pieces of charcoal with a little water. Mix the following ingredients together, and pour the solution slowly over the charcoal so that it is almost completely submerged.

6 tablespoons salt
6 tablespoons bluing
6 tablespoons water
1 tablespoon ammonia

With a medicine dropper, drop different colors of food coloring, ink, or fabric dye over the solution. Within a few hours, interesting crystal shapes of various colors will form. The crystals

will continue to grow for a couple of weeks. Remember, this is one activity that *requires your close supervision.* You want to make sure the bluing, ammonia, and coloring go into the bowl and not into the children's eyes or mouths.

Cutting

Have the children sit by a wastebasket or *in* a large box, and let them use rounded scissors to cut paper, old material, wrapping paper, or magazines.

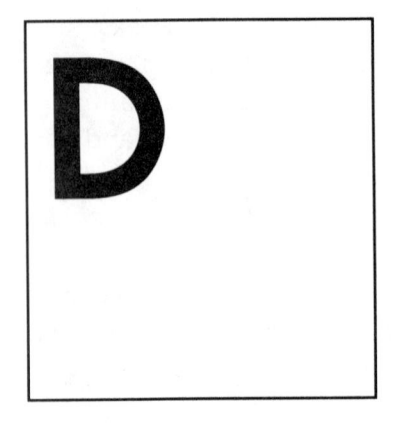

Dancing

I gave the children towels and scarves while I played music. They danced and moved their props quickly or slowly, depending on the tempo of the music. When you do this activity, you may be surprised at the children's performing talent.

Decorator Cans

Save juice or soup cans. Let children glue fabric or construction paper to the cans. Glue lightweight items such as noodles, seeds, and dried beans to the cans. Markers, crayons, and paint are good for adding designs. These make nice gifts for children to give to special people.

Dough Figures

To make play dough, thoroughly mix the ingredients below in the order listed. For easier stirring, keep mixture moist while you mix it. After you add all the ingredients, you might find it necessary to add a little more flour or water to achieve the proper clay consistency.

Mix:
2 cups warm water
2/3 cup oil
1/4 cup liquid soap
food coloring or paint

Add:
5 cups flour
1 cup salt

Give children cookie cutters, butter knives, and small jars, and let them form their own works of art. Place their designs on a cookie sheet, and bake at 350° F for half an hour to one hour, depending on their size. Remember, these dough figures are not edible!

To store unused playdough, place it in a plastic bag, seal tightly, and store at room temperature.

Dress Up

Instead of giving all those old clothes away, I saved a bag for the children. With the clothes, makeup, and a few props, the children created a great atmosphere for a play or for role-playing. By the time they had chosen their clothes, put on their makeup, and decided on a topic for their play, the children had spent the whole morning and had ended up with an extensive production.

Duck, Duck, Goose

This game is an old favorite with energy-filled children. Have the children sit in a circle. One person is the Goose. The Goose goes around the outside of the circle tapping each person on the head, saying "Duck" with each tap. The Goose finally taps someone on the head and says, "Goose." The new Goose runs around the circle chasing the old Goose. The old Goose tries to make it all the way around the circle to the new Goose's place before being tagged. If the old Goose gets tagged, this child is the Goose again. If the old Goose makes it around, the new Goose begins the game again. Make sure that the same child isn't the Goose three or four times in a row.

E

Earphones

If you have a tape recorder or record player with earphones, children will sit quietly for long periods of time listening. Have music available, or tape-record yourself reading one of their favorite books. You control the volume. Make it clear to the children they are not to change the volume. If the children raise the volume too high, they could severely damage their ears.

Easel Painting

A double-sided easel can be one of the best investments you make for the children. One side of the easel is a blackboard with a tray in front to hold chalk and an eraser. The other side is a hardboard to clip paper onto. The tray in front of the hardboard is ideal to store a box of forty-eight crayons, a cup of water, and watercolor paints. Hang an old adult-sized T-shirt on the easel. A child can slip a T-shirt on and off without assistance. Put the easel in an uncarpeted area where spills will be easier to clean up. Place the easel in an area where it can remain up at all times so that children can paint at their leisure.

Eensy Weensy Spider

Do hand motions to this familiar song:

Eensy weensy spider went up the water spout.
Down came the rain and washed the spider out.
Up came the sun and dried out all the rain.
The eensy weensy spider went up the spout again.

Face Masks

Create the children's faces out of aluminum foil. Cut 20" pieces of foil. Fold them in half. Help the children press the foil to their faces. Remove the foil, and with a sharp knife, *you* make slits for eyes, noses, and mouths. Tie string to the sides, and each child has a face mask.

Farmer in the Dell

Children hold hands in a circle for this familiar song. Choose one child to stand in the center and be the farmer as everyone sings the first verse together:

> The farmer in the dell,
> The farmer in the dell,
> Heigh-o the derry-o,
> The farmer in the dell.

Have the farmer choose a wife to stand in the center with him, and sing the second verse:

> The farmer takes a wife,
> The farmer takes a wife,

Heigh-o the derry-o,
The farmer takes a wife.

Continue with the following verses:

The wife takes a child . . .
The child takes a nurse . . .
The nurse takes a dog . . .
The dog takes a cat . . .
The cat takes a rat . . .
The rat takes the cheese . . .
The cheese stands alone . . .

Feelings

One child is chosen to go into another room where the rest of the group can't be heard. The group decides on a mood or feeling such as sad, mad, glad, afraid, hurt, excited, or shy. Each child who remained in the room takes a turn to act out a pantomime of the mood to the child who was out of the room. Props may be used to convey the feeling to the child who is guessing.

Fine Memory

This is one memory game that the children in my day care seemed to really enjoy. I lined three or four objects up on the floor. I worked up to five or six objects as the group seemed ready. I started with familiar objects that were large in size. One child left the room. Another child rearranged the order of the objects. The child returned and tried to put the objects in the original order. I played the game with the children until everyone had a turn.

Finger Paint

1 cup starch
3 cups boiling water
1 cup soap flakes (not powder)
2 tablespoons glycerine
food coloring or powdered tempera paint

Dissolve starch in a little cold water. Add boiling water and stir until thick. Cool slightly and add soap flakes and glycerine. You may want to add a few drops of spice extract or oil of cloves for a pleasing smell. Paint may be divided in small amounts and coloring added. Stir well to avoid lumps. Or give the children uncolored paint, and let them sprinkle in powdered paint.

If you have an oilcloth or a formica-covered table, children can make their designs directly on these. Pieces of paper can be laid on the designs and lifted off. This process gives a different and unusual effect from painting directly on paper. Paint should be kept in covered jars and will keep longer if refrigerated. It can be kept out of the refrigerator for a couple of weeks if spice extract is added.

Flannel Board Stories

I made a flannel board out of a large piece of plywood (heavy corrugated cardboard is OK too). I covered it with felt and secured it firmly with staples and tacks. Next, I colored storybook characters, cut them out, covered them with clear adhesive-backed paper, and then glued felt on the back. I arranged them on a tray in story sequence. I told the children a story while I placed the figures on the flannel board. When I finished, I encouraged the children to tell a story using the characters. I found that coloring books provided a wealth of characters that could be used to make up stories to tell on the flannel board.

Follow the Leader

Let each child have a turn to lead the others on a wild adventure. The leader can walk, jump, hop, crawl, skip, or run. This activity develops large muscle control and entertains at the same time.

Forklift

Have children lie flat on their backs on the floor for this exercise. Have them place their arms above their heads on the floor. They should keep their legs together and lift them up and down just like a forklift. This is a good tummy strengthener!

Fruit Family

I was amazed when I saw how the children played with their fruit families. Take a piece of fabric that measures 30" x 30" and have the child place a grapefruit in the middle. Tie it with yarn to make a head, and let the rest of the fabric hang down for a body. By using various sizes of fruit, you can create a whole family. Let children use markers or crayons to create just the right facial expressions.

Gadget Painting

Various gadgets can be dipped in tempera paint and used to print designs. Place a piece of felt in an aluminum pan and cover it with tempera paint. Let the children dip sponges, bottle tops, or corks into the tempera and create interesting effects on art paper.

Gardening

These gardens are fun and easy to grow. Take a beet, carrot, or white turnip, and cut off most of the vegetable. Leave a small stub and the leafy top. Place the vegetable in a shallow bowl of pebbles and water. Water will suffice if you don't have pebbles. Place the bowl in a sunny area, add water when necessary, and within a few days new sprouts will appear.

Glass Band

Give each child a spoon and a glass with a different amount of liquid in it. As children tap the glasses with their spoons, they'll be surprised at the variety of sounds due to the liquid level in the glasses. Snack time will be ideal for the glass band. As the children drink their juice and play their music, they will hear different tones.

Grass Gardens

Grass in your house? Yes, take a moist sponge, roll it in grass seed, and put the sponge in a saucer of water in a sunny spot. Add water and in a few days you'll see brilliant green grass.

Gravel Mosaic

I helped the children dye gravel. We dropped the stones into shallow tin cans filled with a small amount of tempera paint. After soaking them to just the right color, we scooped the stones onto a newspaper with a metal slotted spoon. While they were drying, the children drew pictures on pieces of cardboard. When the gravel was dry, they glued the colored gravel onto their pictures with thinned white glue.

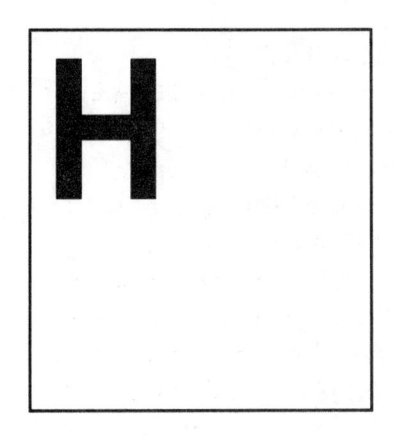

Hammering

I set out hammers, lumber scraps, and 1 1/2" nails with big heads. I made sure there was plenty of space between children. When organizing this activity, show each child how to hold a nail between the thumb and pointer finger. Tap gently to get the nail started, then it's OK to hit harder. Make sure the child's fingers are out of the way and he or she isn't holding the hammer too close to the hammer's head.

Hand in the Bag

Place various objects such as an apple, banana, feather, book, and a ball in a bag. Choose objects of different size, texture, and weight. Have the children take turns placing their hands in the bag and by touch alone guessing what is in the bag.

Happy House

This activity combines art along with storytelling. Talk as a group about things that make us happy, scared, sad, or mad. Give children each a large piece of construction paper. Help each child draw an outline of a big house. Ask children to cut or tear pictures from magazines that illustrate one of the feelings. Have children paste the pictures inside the houses. Have children take turns explaining their pictures and telling what feelings the pictures show.

Hickory Dickory Dock

Recite this well-known nursery rhyme with children.

Allow children to make up hand motions or body movements.

Hickory dickory dock.
The mouse ran up the clock.
The clock struck one,
The mouse ran down.
Hickory dickory dock.

Hide and Seek

Before beginning this game, designate one child to be "It." "It" counts very slowly to ten, while the other children hide. The children who hide try to run back to the "free" space where "It" was counting. The children who reach the free space before being tagged are not "It." The first child tagged before getting to the "free" space is the next person to be "It." The children should be allowed to hide only in a limited area so that nobody becomes lost. A confined area also gives younger or slower children a chance to hide. Make sure all children understand the boundaries.

Hot Cross Buns

Here's an old familiar song to sing with the children:

Hot cross buns,
Hot cross buns;
One a-penny, two a-penny,
Hot cross buns.

Hot Potato

Have the children sit in a circle on the floor. Turn on the radio. While the radio is playing, roll a ball from one child to another as fast as possible. When the music stops, the child who is holding the ball is out. The circle closes in until there are only two children left and then finally a winner.

Humpty Dumpty

Humpty Dumpty sat on a wall,
Humpty Dumpty had a great fall.
All the king's horses
And all the king's men
Couldn't put Humpty together again.

Have the children sit on the floor with pillows behind them. As you say the second line, allow the children to fall back on their pillows.

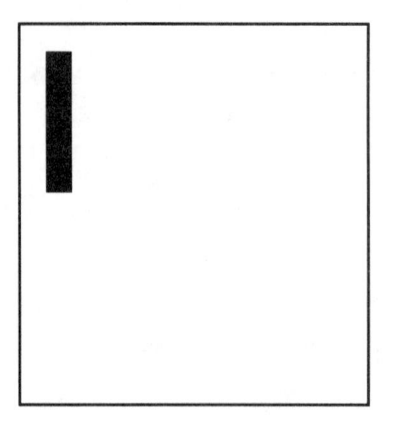

Ice Cream Cone Cupcakes

This is one activity the children love. Heat the oven to 400° F. Mix a cake mix according to the directions on the package. Place flat-bottomed ice cream cones on a cookie sheet, and fill them half full. If you put in too much or too little batter, the cones won't have a nicely rounded top. Bake the cupcakes for the amount of time suggested on the cake mix box. After the cupcakes have cooled, give each of the children a serving of frosting and some sprinkles. They will enjoy frosting, decorating, and admiring more than eating.

I See the Moon

I see the moon and the moon sees me.
The moon sees the one that I want to see.
God bless the moon and God bless me.
And God bless the one that I want to see.

Allow children to make up motions for this song.

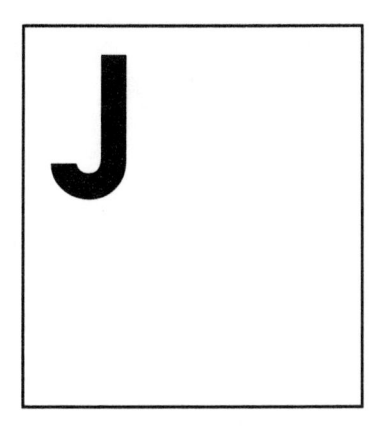

Jack and Jill

Jack and Jill went up the hill
To fetch a pail of water,
Jack fell down and broke his crown,
And Jill came tumbling after.

Have the children make up some actions to go with this familiar song.

Jumping Beans

Here's a good activity to get the children moving in the morning. Choose a grassy spot outdoors, and have the children jump on two feet from one designated spot to another and then back again. After the children jump, point out that they are breathing harder and their hearts are really pumping. Explain that our hearts work harder when we work harder.

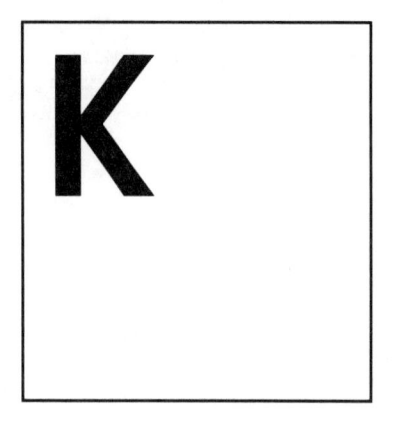

Key Holders

Each child needs a 6" x 10" piece of stained or painted wood about 3/4" thick. Make four to six nail holes in each board. Let children glue pictures to the boards. Monitor the amount of glue used. Wipe the excess off with a damp cloth. After the glue has dried, let the children paint a clear protective coating over their entire piece of wood. Then have them screw hooks into the nail holes. Help them attach picture hangers to the back.

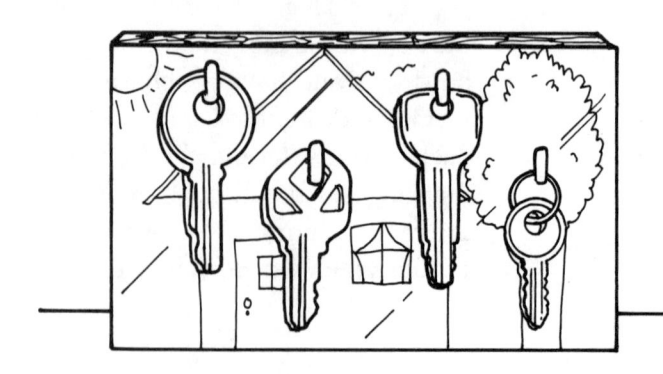

Kick It, Roll It, Bounce It

Allow children the opportunity to experiment with ball handling. Let each child try to improve his or her skill. Form teams and have individual races.

Kitty in the Corner

This game is played with five children. Choose one child to stand in the middle of the room, while the others select a corner of the room and stand in it. When you say, "Kitty wants a corner," all the children run to different corners and the "kitty" in the middle tries to get a corner. The child left without a corner becomes the one in the middle. Make sure nobody is the "kitty" more than three or four times in a row.

Little Miss Muffet

Children can dramatize this familar rhyme.

Little Miss Muffet sat on a tuffet,
Eating some curds and whey;
Along came a spider,
And sat down beside her,
And frightened Miss Muffet away.

London Bridge

London Bridge is falling down,
Falling down, falling down.
London Bridge is falling down,
My fair Lady O.

Have two children form a bridge by facing each other and raising their clasped hands. Others can walk under the bridge while saying the verse together.

Long and Short

Have children spread out and stand in a line. Stand in front of the children, several feet away from them. Spread your arms out wide to indicate "long" and bring your hands close together to indicate "short." The children need to take the same size steps as your hands indicate while moving toward you.

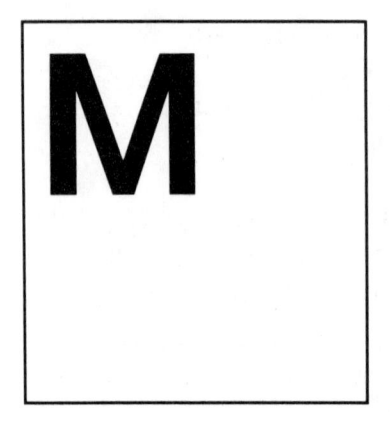

Magnets

Provide one or more magnets. Gather together a collection of different types of materials such as a nail, stainless steel spoon, rubber band, pencil, cloth, mug, aluminum foil, tin can, safety pin, a glass, paper clip, cotton swab, and a plastic bowl. Let the children try to pick up the items with the magnet. Note that the magnet will not attract all of the items. Tell the children to sort the items into two piles according to whether the magnet picked them up or not. After the experiment mix up the two piles, and ask the children which items the magnet attracted and which items it didn't.

Magnifying

Let each child examine a piece of toast, a drop of milk, a seed, a speck of dirt, a rock, a piece of paper, or his or her shirt or finger under a magnifying glass.

Makeup

They all love it! Even the boys enjoy dabbling in makeup. The powder makeup is easy to put on and can be wiped off with a tissue. After children have finished their artistic endeavors, they can join in a game of make-believe. Let the children choose what character they want to be. They could be a clown, a lady, a bum, or anything else their imaginations can dream of. It's fun to see children critique each other's makeup and suggest what role others should assume.

Markers

Children enjoy coloring with markers. The colors are vivid and easy to use. They must be one of our best inventions. The color flows so easily and the markers respond so well that children feel successful when using them. It is better to buy markers with fat tips and large cases. And, *be sure they are water based.* Newspaper on the table is a must because it's hard for children to confine themselves to the paper. If they make a mistake and draw where they are not supposed to, remove the ink with a strong detergent. The caps should be put on the pens immediately after use. If the markers do dry up, it's possible to rejuvenate them with a ten-minute soak in a cup of warm water. Waterproof pens need denatured alcohol or nail polish remover to bring them back to life. This will also remove traces of marker left on the walls or floor. Do not use denatured alcohol or nail polish remover on any type of fabric.

Mary Had a Little Lamb

Children can dramatize this familiar song.

Mary had a little lamb,
Little lamb, little lamb,
Mary had a little lamb,
Its fleece was white as snow.

Everywhere that Mary went,
Mary went, Mary went,
Everywhere that Mary went,
The lamb was sure to go.

Material Collage

Save all your old scraps of material, yarn, and ribbon. Give the children rounded scissors, and let them cut various sizes and shapes to glue onto construction paper or cardboard.

Mummy

Save your old rags or sheets, and tear them into strips. Let the children wrap each other up in the strips. They can also construct a play around their novel costumes.

Musical Chairs

Let the children set up the chairs. They should line up one less chair than the number of people playing the game. The children move around the chairs while music is playing. You can use the radio, a record, or a tape. When the music stops, the children must all find empty chairs and sit down. One child will be left without a chair; that person must sit out to the side. A chair is removed and the game continues until only one child is left.

My Name Is

This song will help children learn their names, ages, and the name of the city where they live. Have them sit in a circle while everyone chants the song. You point to a child when it's his or her turn to complete a sentence.

My name is <u>Joan.</u>
I am <u>three</u> years old.
I live on <u>Apple</u> Street.
I live in <u>L.A.</u>
My brother's name is <u>John.</u>
I have a <u>cat.</u>
My favorite toy is a <u>tricycle.</u>

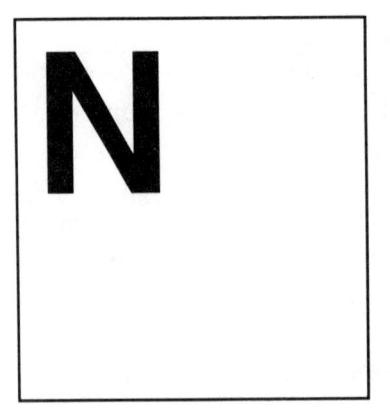

Nature Walks

Short walks are a fun way to expose children to the world around them. Have the children look for a squirrel, listen to a bird, or find a bird's nest. Let them collect leaves, small branches, and rocks in a paper bag. Then the children bring the treasures back to glue onto pieces of paper or cardboard.

Noodle Collage

Have children glue noodles of various colors, sizes, and shapes on pieces of paper or cardboard. Variations of noodle creativity are endless.

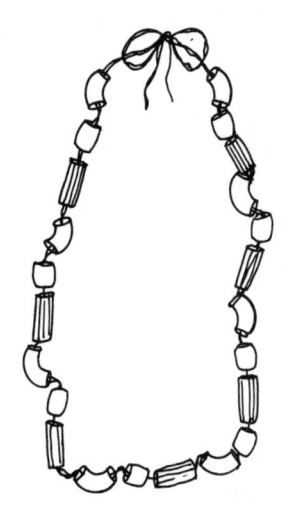

Noodle Necklace

Wind clear adhesive around the ends of pieces of yarn or string so that children can thread noodles more easily. Use the necklaces as birthday presents or as props for a play. While the children are stringing their necklaces, they can be creating their own plays or deciding on a favorite story to act out.

Numbers

Save last year's calendars. They are great for cutting-and-pasting projects. Let the children cut out numbers from one to twenty. They can glue the numbers in order as you count either as a group or individually.

Nuts of the World

It is hard to believe how many things can be made out of nutshells. Half a walnut can be a boat, a basket, the body for a turtle, or a mask. Peanut shells make good caterpillars. Almonds turn into great bugs. Use clay to form the legs for the turtle, caterpillar, or bug. Be sure to clean the shells well before beginning the projects.

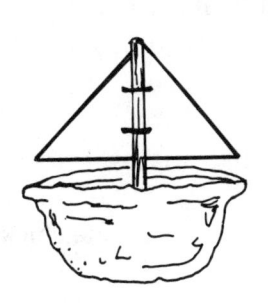

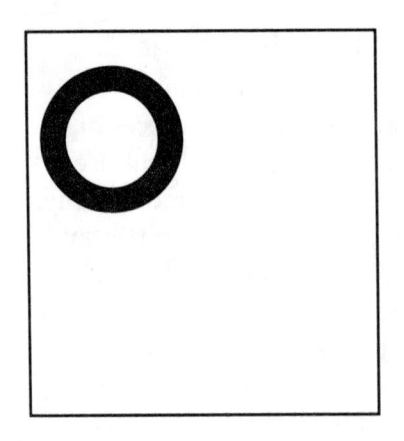

Obstacle Course

Have the children pool their ideas and set up an obstacle course. They can go over a chair, under a table, around a tree, etc.

Old MacDonald Had a Farm

This old favorite is loved by all children. Everyone wants to be involved.

Old MacDonald had a farm,
Ee-igh, ee-igh, oh.
And on that farm he had some chicks.
Ee-igh, ee-igh, oh.

Chorus:
With a cluck, cluck here.
And a cluck, cluck there.
Here a cluck.
There a cluck.
Everywhere a cluck, cluck.
Old MacDonald had a farm,
Ee-igh, ee-igh, oh.

Repeat verse using:
duck—quack
turkey—gobble
pig—oink
cow—moo
donkey—hee-haw

1, 2, 3, 4, 5

1, 2, 3, 4, 5
I caught a fish alive.
Why did you let him go?
Because he bit my finger so
OUCH!

The children think this song is great because they can almost scream the "OUCH" at the end.

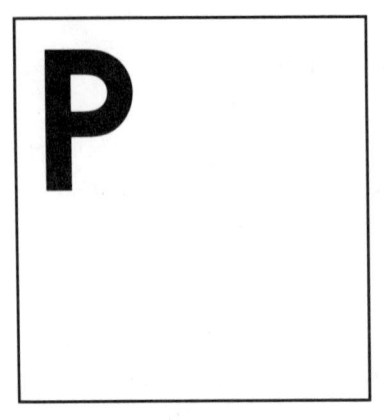

Paper Collage

Children are intrigued with paper of different colors and textures. Provide them with paper, rounded scissors, and glue. Watch their imaginations go into motion without any suggestions or ideas from you.

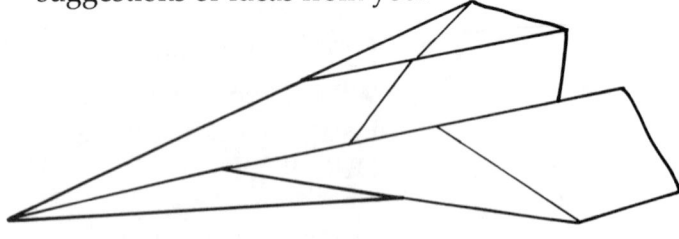

Peanut Butter Balls

3 tablespoons honey
4 tablespoons peanut butter
1/2 cup nonfat dry milk
1/4 cup dry cereal flakes

Mix peanut butter and honey. Slowly add nonfat dry milk. Mix well. Have the children grease their hands and form balls. Roll the balls in the dry cereal flakes. Chill until firm. Makes 18 balls.

Peanut Hunt

Before the children arrive, hide peanuts in an outside area that is contained. You want to be sure the children don't wander off. Arm children with paper bags, and let them begin their great hunt.

Place Mats

Let the children make a set of place mats. They make great gifts. Seasonal mats are unique and a good learning experience for the children. Have children cut pictures that depict a season of the year from magazines. They can then glue the pictures onto construction paper. Spray the place mats with hair spray for more durability.

Pop! Goes the Weasel

All around the cobbler's bench,
The monkey chased the weasel,
The monkey thought 'twas all in fun.
Pop! Goes the weasel.
A penny for a spool of thread,
A penny for a needle,
That's the way the money goes,
Pop! Goes the weasel.

Popcorn

Popcorn is easy to make and tastes so good. Children like to watch and listen to the popcorn popping. Give each child a paper cup filled halfway with popcorn. Show children where the trash is, so when they are finished, they can throw their own cups away. Then lead the children outside or to a table to enjoy the treats.

Popsicles

Pour juice into individual cups. Flavored yogurt will also work. It tastes similar to creamy ice cream. Place the individual cups in the freezer. When the liquid begins to freeze, insert plastic spoons into the centers. Put the cups back into the freezer until they are frozen solid. When the children are ready to dive into their master-pieces, take them outside. Give each child the cup the popsicle was frozen in so that there will be a place to put the popsicle if a distraction arises.

Punch a Plastic Bag

Plastic punching bags are inexpensive and may be bought at toy stores and many drug stores. These bags make great targets for kids who need to vent their emotions. If you see children who are having problems, direct them to the bag and explain that it is OK to hit, kick, or lay on the punching bag, but they must keep their hands off the other children. Encourage children to vigorously "beat up on" the bag!

Puppet Show

I dug out my old greeting cards and let the children pick out their favorites and attach them to popsicle sticks. A stapler provided the most secure way of fastening the card to the stick, although it would have been easier for children to use glue or tape. After assembling the puppets, I encouraged the children to do a puppet show. Be sensitive to the needs of the children in your care. If the children are interested in giving a performance, let each child give an original show with one or two puppets. Later the children may work in pairs, or the whole group can work on one simple story or nursery rhyme.

Push Pull Toys

These toys come in bright colors and often make a noise when they are pulled, which are definite attractions for small children.

Q-Tip Painting

Provide the children with paper, small containers of tempera paint, and Q-Tips. Show children how to dip the ends of the Q-Tips in the paint and then use them to make designs on the paper.

Rain, Rain Go Away

Children can repeat this rhyme on a rainy day.

Rain, rain, go away
Come again another day.
Little Johnny wants to play.
Rain, rain go away.

Raisin Nut Roll

1 1/2 cups raisins
1/2 cup peanuts
pinch of salt

Combine the raisins and peanuts. Put them through a food chopper. Mix well and add salt. With greased hands, let the children mold the mixture into interesting shapes. Chill their designs and slice.

Record Player

Children enjoy listening to nursery rhymes, fairy tales, or music during quiet times. Sometimes it's difficult for the children to calm down. So, listening to a record allows them the time to unwind and gives them something to do.

Ring Around the Rosie

Children can walk, run, or skip in a circle while repeating this rhyme.

Ring around the rosie
Pocketful of posies
Ashes, ashes
We all fall down.

Rock-a-Bye Baby

Children can dramatize this familiar song.

Rock-a-bye, baby, in the tree top,
When the wind blows, the cradle will rock;
When the bough breaks, the cradle will fall,
And down will come baby, cradle and all.

Rocks

Send children outside on a fun rock hunt. When the children come back with their various rocks, let them design marvelous pictures on them using colorful felt-tipped pens. Have children wear old T-shirts to protect their clothing before beginning. By using epoxy or a strong adhesive glue, they'll be able to glue smaller rocks onto larger rocks and form interesting shapes. The artistic rocks can then be used as accent pieces in their rooms or as gifts for someone special.

Rubber Man

This is a good exercise that provides children a chance to stretch their muscles. Have children imagine that they are rubber men and that their bodies can stretch up to the ceiling and to the right and left. As the children imagine how flexible they are, have them actually stretch in every direction.

Sad Puppy

This is a simple game the children love and remember. One child is picked to be the puppy. The rest of the group sits on the floor in an informal circle. The puppy crawls on all fours and sadly stops by each person to say, "Bowwow." That person must pat the puppy on the head and say "nice puppy" without the trace of a smile. The first person to smile, laugh, or giggle becomes the new puppy. The puppy's mood can change from lonely to hungry or angry.

Sanding

Give children some sandpaper and some pieces of wood. Allow children to sand the edges of the wood until they feel smooth. Sanding teaches the difference between rough and smooth. Let children touch the rough spots before and after sanding.

Screwing

Nail one or two blocks to a workbench ahead of time. Hammer nails far enough into the blocks to make holes for the screws. Remove the nails. Show the children how to screw in a screw. Tell them to start the screw with their fingers. Once the screw has started, have them take turns holding the bottom part of the screwdriver with their fingers to keep it on the screw. Have each child hold the handle of the screwdriver in the other hand and begin to slowly turn it.

Shadow Boxes

Use old shoe box lids. The children can cover the inside of the lids with construction paper, paint, or crayons. They can glue shells, leaves, twigs, seeds, bugs, or whatever they would like inside the lids. Add finishing touches with crayons or markers. Stretch clear plastic wrap around the box lids to make "glass" fronts. Carefully tape the plastic to the back of the lids.

Shape Collage

Stack many pieces of construction paper on top of each other, and cut rectangles, circles, triangles, and squares ranging in size from 1" to 4". Show the children how to make a car with two circles and a rectangle. Adding a thinner rectangle makes a handle, and the car becomes a wagon. The children can glue the shapes on pieces of paper.

Shaving Cream Painting

This activity brings out the true artist in all. Spray nonmentholated shaving cream on a vinyl-covered table. Add a little food coloring and watch a Picasso unfold before your eyes. This is one of those activities that allows the children complete freedom of expression because shaving cream is so much fun to touch. Have the children try to make designs using their fingers, hands, elbows, or feet! Combs, toothbrushes, or sticks may also be used for unusual effects.

Simon Says

This popular and valuable game teaches children to lead, follow, and listen. Each child should be given the opportunity to lead the group, while the others listen to the leader and follow the directions. The leader gives a direction such as *Simon says, "Take one step forward."* The others follow the direction every time it is preceded by the words, "Simon says." If the leader does not say, "Simon says," the others must remain where they are. If someone moves to follow the direction, that person must go back to the starting line. The first child to reach Simon is the next leader.

Smells Like

Choose a variety of foods with distinctive odors, such as an onion, a lemon, peppermint, pepper, cinnamon, vanilla, or bubble gum. Let the children look at the items, and then blindfold them and let them try to identify each item by smell only.

Sponge Painting

Dampen a small sponge in water. Have the child dip the damp sponge into tempera paint and blot it on a plain piece of paper.

Squirting Plastic Bottles

Fill empty plastic squirt bottles with water. On warm days let children water your plants and themselves!

Stained-Glass Window

Help children grate colored crayon onto a piece of newspaper. Cut two 12" squares of waxed paper. Cover an ironing board with newspaper to keep it clean. Lay one square of waxed paper on the newspaper. Sprinkle the crayon shavings on the waxed paper. Place the second piece of waxed paper over the crayon shavings. Cover the waxed paper with more newspaper. Press the paper with a warm iron for the children until the crayon shavings are melted. Trim the edges and hang by a string in front of a sunny window.

String Paint

This is a good outside project. Have children dip pieces of string into tempera paint. Let them pull the strings across paper to make various designs.

Styrofoam Puppet

This type of puppet is lasting and easy to assemble. The children can be as detail oriented as they want. Have children decorate 6" Styrofoam balls to resemble faces. They can use buttons for the eyes, raisins for noses, and yarn can be attached with pins for some hair. Mouths can be drawn with marking pens. After children finish the faces, they put fabric squares over popsicle sticks and push them up into the balls. A popsicle stick under the fabric makes a handle for a child to hold on to. This handle will come in handy if a child chooses to do a dramatic presentation with the puppet.

Sweet Potato

Sweet potatoes grow into beautiful vines. Put four toothpicks in a circle around a potato about halfway down. Place the pointed end of the potato into a glass or jar of water so that the toothpicks rest on the rim of the glass. Keep it in a sunny area and add water when necessary; within two weeks you'll see new growth.

Sweets and Sours

Let the children sample familiar foods and describe the taste. The children probably won't say whether the taste is sweet or sour, but they may say the taste is good or bad. When playing the tasting game, emphasize that they shouldn't try unfamiliar foods unless they've asked an adult if the food is safe to eat. Let the children experiment with unsweetened chocolate, salt, lemon, brown sugar, pineapple, and unbuttered white bread.

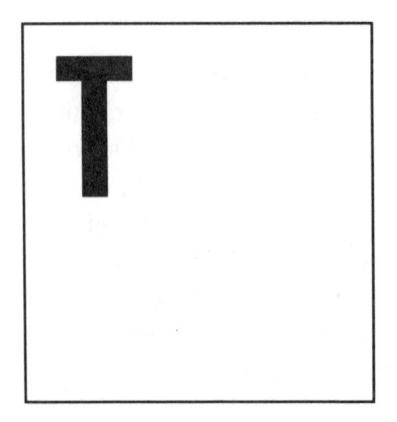

Tape Recorder

A tape recorder can be used in a novel way for young children because most of them have never heard their own voices before. Have the children rehearse songs or practice saying their names, ages, addresses, and other pertinent facts. Then have them speak into the tape recorder. This will help teach the children self-confidence and will also help them to speak clearly. Play the tape back, and ask the children if they recognize their own voices.

Telephone

Attach soup cans to both ends of a long string. Let the children demonstrate answering the telephone. It's easy to guide this activity and use it to teach good telephone manners.

Tempera Paints

I used various techniques with tempera, although they had to be closely supervised. Tempera paints may be purchased premixed, in powder form, or as a condensed liquid. If you buy powder or condensed tempera, mix it by using equal parts of starch and liquid detergent instead of water. The starch gives the paint substance and the liquid detergent has built-in cleaning power to prevent stains, should the paint spill on the children's clothing. Add a small amount of liquid detergent to the premixed tempera for the same protection against stains.

Tent a Table

Children love cozy places and this activity is great for indoor rainy days. Give the children an old sheet, and let them tent a table. With an old sheet and a table, they immediately have a playhouse. The playhouse is just the beginning of a day of fantasy. Add dolls to the tent, and it becomes a house. Add cars and trucks, and the tent can be a garage. Dig out some blocks, and the children can pretend it's a building site. With

very few suggestions from you, children will be
actively creating all day long. Their playhouse
can also act as a prop for a stage play. Encourage
the children to use their imaginations to turn
their playtime into a production they can share
with you and each other.

This Old Man

This old man, he played one,
He played knick knack on my thumb.

Chorus:
With a knick knack paddy wack,
Give your dog a bone,
This old man came rolling home.

This old man, he played two,
He played knick knack on my shoe.
chorus

This old man, he played three,
He played knick knack on my knee.
chorus

This old man, he played four,
He played knick knack on my door.
chorus

This old man, he played five,
He played knick knack on my hive.
chorus

This old man, he played six,
He played knick knack on my sticks.
chorus

This old man, he played seven,
He played knick knack up to heaven.
chorus

This old man, he played nine,
He played knick knack on my line.
chorus

This old man, he played ten,
He played knick knack over again.
chorus

Transfers

Have each child fold a piece of paper in half
and color the inside left page completely with
crayon. Fold the paper and have the child draw a
picture with a pencil on the front page. The
drawing will be transferred in color on the inside
right page.

Twinkle, Twinkle, Little Star

Twinkle, twinkle, little star,
How I wonder what you are.
Up above the world so high,
Like a diamond in the sky.
Twinkle, twinkle, little star,
How I wonder what you are.

Under, Over

Play some lively music while the children go under and over items set up in an obstacle course. When the music stops, the children must also stop. Have them each tell if they are under or over the object at which they are stopped. Then begin the music again and continue the game.

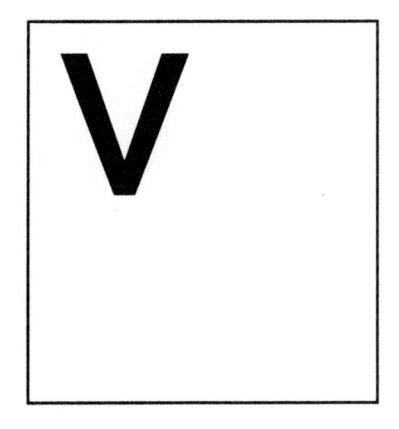

Vanishing Object

Place five or six items on a tray. Children sit in a circle and view the items on the tray. Then they hide their eyes. Ask one child to remove one thing from the tray. The others open their eyes and try to guess what has vanished. The game continues until each child has had a chance to remove an item. As the children get used to the process, add more items to the tray. I was amazed at how much they could remember.

Vegetable Printing

Cut up pieces of vegetables such as potatoes or carrots. Let the children make marks with rounded scissors or some other blunt instrument on the cut vegetables. Then they can press the vegetables onto a piece of felt that has been saturated with tempera paint and stamp the vegetables onto paper to make prints.

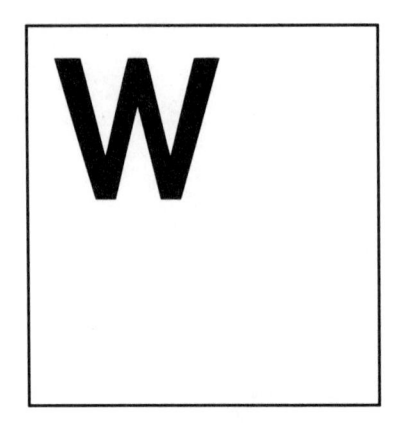

Watercolor Paints

These paints are ideal because they wash out of clothing and are easy to clean off the floor. I bought the more expensive watercolors so that the children could view their artwork in vivid color.

Water Painting

Fill a bucket or large pan with water. Give children big paintbrushes, and let them paint everything in sight. This activity is usually very popular because it gives children so much freedom.

What If . . .

Sit in a circle and talk about what would happen in emergency situations. Ask the children what they would do if . . .

. . . they saw a hurt rabbit.

. . . they smelled smoke in the house.

. . . they saw a stranger standing at the front door.

. . . their mothers were choking.

. . . their brothers or sisters had cut knees.

. . . the water pipe under the sink were broken.

. . . their baby sisters or brothers ate furniture polish.

. . . a stranger offered them candy.

After the children express their feelings and ideas, you can add practical advice.

What's That Noise?

I chose sounds that the children were familiar with, such as two pot lids banging together, a pencil sharpener, a can opener, a garbage disposal, a door closing, and water running. Each child demonstrated one of the sounds by closing a door or turning on a faucet, and so on. The children then covered their eyes while I made the sounds. The children tried to guess the sound.

Wheel Toys

All children love wheel toys. Don't worry about having enough toys to go around. Rather, make it clear to the children that it's important to learn to share and wait for a turn. You and the children can organize different games that give everyone something to do while they wait for a turn. Some of the children who wait for a turn can pretend to work in a service station, and the drivers can come to put gas in their cars. Others can be storekeepers. Another child could be a parking lot attendant and give parking tickets to those who go in and out. You can be the police officer who tickets reckless drivers or speeders. Issue warnings, followed by tickets, to those who ride improperly or bump into objects or their friends. If a child gets a ticket, that ends his or her turn. This game teaches children the proper way to ride a wheel toy. You may want to explain that these same rules apply to adults when they drive. When children are finished with the wheel toys, they should drive them back into the parking lot. Remember to rotate jobs and turns on the wheel toys equally. Sometimes it is still difficult for children to wait for a turn to ride a wheel toy. A kitchen timer will come in handy for giving each rider a fair turn.

Windmill

Have the children stretch their arms out to their sides about shoulder height. Have them move their arms around and around like windmills. Then have the children reverse the direction of their arms.

Wooden Puzzles

Use puzzles that have no more than five pieces. A helpful secret is to color the back of each puzzle piece. Make the backs of all pieces belonging to one puzzle the same color. When you're sorting five or six puzzles, it's easier to sort them by the color on the back than the partial puzzle picture on the front.

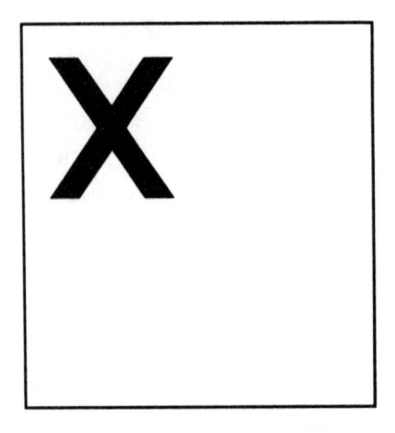

Xylophone

I played the musical scale from low to high on a children's piano or xylophone. Then I sang the scale using *do re mi fa so la ti do*. I moved my hand up as my voice went up. Together we sang the scale as I played it. I let each child try singing the scale as I played it. Then each child had a turn to play the scale, while the others moved their hands up as the sound went up. Then we played a game. I played two notes. The children indicated with their hands whether the second note was higher or lower than the first. Each child took a turn playing two or three notes going up or down the scale. The others showed the up or down movement with their hands.

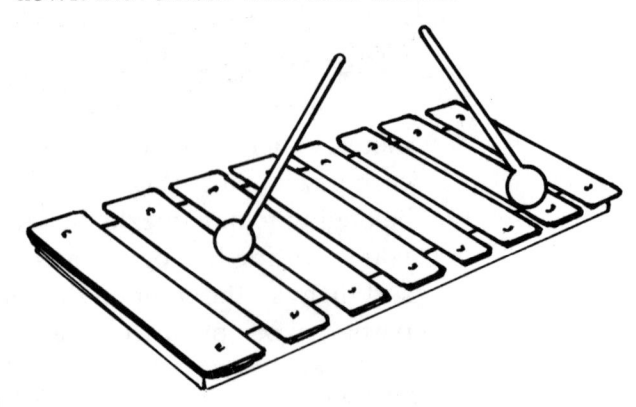

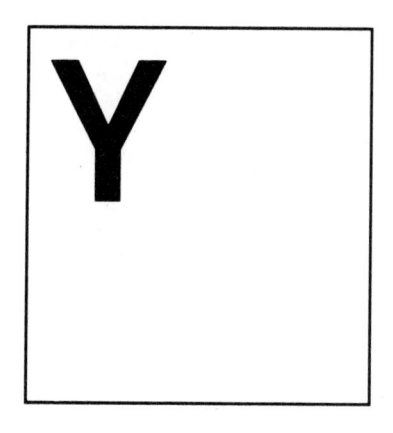

Yarn Designs

Provide each child with a 12" x 12" piece of wood. The wood may be painted or stained ahead of time. Let children hammer nails partway into their boards. Then let them make designs by wrapping yarn around the nails. Rubber bands could also be stretched across the nails.

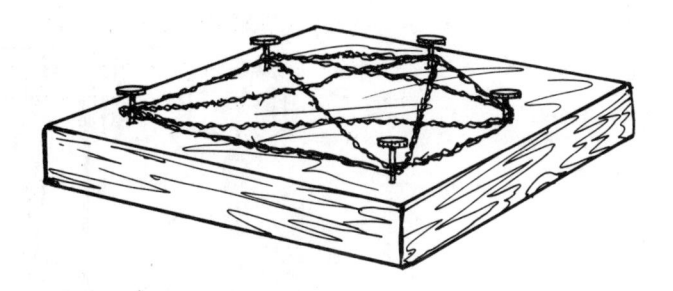

Z

Zippers

Allowing children the opportunity to zip a zipper is a great small motor activity. Sew a zipper in the center of a square piece of fabric. On the side of a box, cut out a piece of cardboard a little smaller than the piece of fabric. Replace the missing cardboard with the piece of fabric with the zipper. Repeat on the other three sides of the box. Children can practice zipping on all four sides of the box.

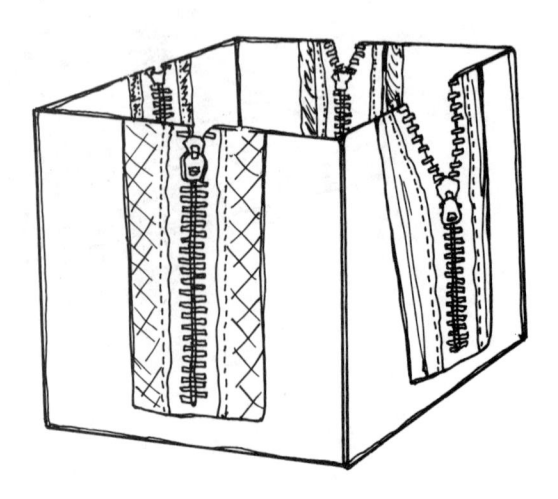

Zero, Blastoff!

This is a good exercise for generating enthusiasm. Count backward from ten down to one. As you count aloud, the children slowly go from a standing to a squatting position, so that they are all the way down by the time you reach number one. Tell the children that when you say, "Zero, Blastoff!" they are to jump up as high as they can, as if they were rockets blasting off. Try counting at different speeds, and have the children match the speed of their movements with your counting. They might also enjoy shouting, "Zero, Blastoff!" with you.

Recommended Books for Preschool-age Children

Beall, Pamela, and Susan Nipp. *Wee Sing.* Los Angeles: Price Stern Sloan, 1983.

Bridwell, Norman. *Clifford the Big Red Dog.* New York: Scholastic, 1963.

Brown, Margaret Wise. *Important Book.* New York: Harper & Row, 1949.

Bruna, Dick. *I Know About Numbers.* New York: Methuen, 1981.

Burningham, John. *Where's Julius?* New York: Crown, 1986.

Burton, Virginia Lee. *Choo Choo.* Boston: Houghton Mifflin, 1937.

———. *Mike Mulligan and His Steam Shovel.* Boston: Houghton Mifflin, 1939.

Clifton, Lucille. *Everett Anderson's Nine Months Long.* New York: Holt, 1978.

Conford, Ellen. *Eugene the Brave.* Boston: Little, Brown, 1978.

DeBrunhoff, Jean. *Babar's Anniversary Album.* New York: Random House, 1981.

Duvoisin, Roger. *Importance of Crocus.* New York: Knopf, 1981.

Flack, Marjorie. *Ask Mr. Bear.* New York: Macmillan,1932.

———. *Story About Ping.* New York: Viking, 1933.

Freeman, Don. *Bearymore*. New York: Viking, 1976.

——— . *Corduroy*. New York: Viking, 1968.

——— . *Pocket for Corduroy*. New York: Viking, 1978.

Gackenbach, Dick. *Hound and Bear*. New York: Clarion, 1976.

Galdone, Paul. *Henny Penny*. New York: Clarion, 1968.

——— . *Little Red Hen*. New York: Clarion, 1973.

Gramatky, Hardie. *Little Toot*. New York: Putnam, 1981.

Hoban, Russel. *Bedtime for Frances*. New York: Harper & Row, 1960.

Hoban, Tana. *Is It Rough? Is It Smooth? Is It Shiny?* New York: Greenwillow, 1984.

Howe, James. *There's a Monster Under My Bed*. New York: Atheneum, 1986.

Hutchins, Pat. *Don't Forget the Bacon*. New York: Greenwillow, 1976.

Johnson, Crockett. *Harold and the Purple Crayon*. New York: Harper & Row, 1955.

Keats, Ezra Jack. *Jennie's Hat*. New York: Harper & Row, 1966.

——— . *Pet Show*. New York: Macmillan, 1972.

Kellogg, Steven. *Mystery of the Missing Red Mitten* , New York: Dial, 1974.

——— . *Pinkerton Behave*. New York: Dial, 1979.

Kraus, Ruth. *Carrot Seed*. New York: Harper & Row, 1945.

Lionni, Leo. *Alexander and the Wind-up Mouse*. New York: Knopf, 1969.

——— . *Frederick*. New York: Knopf, 1967.

——— . *It's Mine*. New York: Knopf, 1986.

Lobel, Arnold. *Treeful of Pigs*. New York: Greenwillow, 1979.

———. *Zoo for Mister Muster*. New York: Harper & Row, 1962.

Marshall, James. *George and Martha*. Boston: Houghton Mifflin, 1972.

Mayer, Mercer. *There's an Alligator Under My Bed*. New York: Dial, 1987.

McCloskey, Robert. *Blueberries for Sal*. New York: Viking, 1948.

———. *Make Way for Ducklings*. New York: Viking, 1941.

Prestine, Joan. *My Special Feelings*. Los Angeles: Price Stern Sloan, 1987.

Rey, H. A. *Curious George*. Boston: Houghton Mifflin, 1941.

Sendak, Maurice. *Chicken Soup with Rice*. New York: Harper & Row, 1962.

———. *Where the Wild Things Are*. New York: Harper & Row, 1963.

Seuss, Dr. *The Cat in the Hat*. New York: Random House, 1957.

———. *Green Eggs and Ham*. New York: Random House, 1960.

———. *One Fish, Two Fish, Red Fish, Blue Fish*. New York: Beginner, 1960.

Steig, William. *Doctor De Soto*. New York: Farrar, Straus and Giroux, 1982.

Titherington, Jeanne. *Pumpkin, Pumpkin*. New York: Greenwillow, 1986.

Viorst, Judith. *Alexander and the Terrible, Horrible, No Good, Very Bad Day*. New York: Atheneum, 1972.

Waber, Bernard. *Lyle, Lyle, Crocodile*. Boston: Houghton Mifflin, 1965.

Suggested Reading

Activities

Painter, Genevieve. *Teach Your Baby*. New York: Simon and Schuster, 1971.

Art and Crafts

Arnold, Arnold. *The Crowell Book of Arts and Crafts for Children*. New York: Crowell, 1975.

Klimo, Joan. *What Can I Do Today?* New York: Pantheon, 1971.

Lowenfeld, Viktor. *Your Child and His Art*. New York: Macmillan, 1954.

Sunset Books and Sunset Magazine Staff. *Children's Crafts*. Menlo Park, CA.: Sunset Books and Sunset Magazine, 1978.

Child Development

Dobson, James. *Dare to Discipline*. Wheaton, IL: Tyndale House, 1970.

——— . *The Strong-Willed Child*. Wheaton, IL: Tyndale House, 1978.

Eden, Alvin. *Positive Parenting*. New York: Bobbs-Merrill, 1980.

Gesell, Arnold, M.D. *The First Five Years of Life*. New York: Harper & Row, 1940.

Gordon, Thomas, M.D. *Parent Effectiveness Training*. New York: Wyden, 1970.

Hunter, Madeline. *Improving Your Child's Behavior*. St. Louis: Bowman, 1971.

Ilg, Frances, M.D., and Louise Ames of the Gesell Institute. *Child Behavior from Birth to Ten*. New York: Harper & Row, 1955.

Leach, Penelope. *Your Baby and Child*. New York: Knopf, 1978.

Shedd, Charlie. *You Can Be a Great Parent*. Waco, TX: Word Books, 1970.

Weisberger, Eleanor. *Your Young Child and You*. New York: Dutton, 1975.

Zink, J., Ph.D. *Champions in the Making. Book One: Building Positive Self-Concept in Kids*. Box 3279, Manhattan Beach, CA 90266, 1981.

————. *Champions in the Making. Book Two: Motivating Kids*. Box 3279, Manhattan Beach, CA 90266, 1983.

Day Care

Fein, Greta. *Day Care in Context*. New York: Wiley, 1973.

Education

Ames, Louise. *Don't Push Your Preschooler*. New York: Harper & Row, 1974.

Kranyik, Margery. *Starting School*. New York: Continuum, 1982.

Music and Dance

Hunter, Hilda. *Growing Up with Music*. Old Tappan, NJ: Hewitt House, 1970.

Maynard, Olga. *Children and Dance and Music*. New York: Scribner, 1968.

Index

Toys

Woodworking